UROPTERYX

Written and Illustrated by
Michael W. Skrepnick

MYSTERIOUS FEATHERED DINOSAUR

Enslow Elementary, an imprint of Enslow Publishers, Inc.

Enslow Elementary® is a registered trademark of Enslow Publishers, Inc.
Copyright © 2005 by Enslow Publishers, Inc.

Library of Congress Cataloging-in-Publication Data

Skrepnick, Michael William.
    Sinosauropteryx—mysterious feathered dinosaur / Michael W. Skrepnick.
        p. cm. — (I like dinosaurs!)
    Includes bibliographical references and index.
    ISBN-10: 0-7660-2623-X
    1. Sinosauropteryx—Juvenile literature. I. Title.
    QE862.S3S485 2005
    567.912—dc22

                                        2004016788

ISBN-13: 978-0-7660-2623-0

Printed in the United States of America

10 9 8 7 6 5 4 3 2

Series Literacy Consultant:

Allan A. De Fina, Ph.D.
Past President of the New Jersey Reading Association
Professor, Department of Literacy Education
New Jersey City University

Science Consultant:

Philip J. Currie, Ph.D.
Curator of Dinosaur Research
Royal Tyrrell Museum
Alberta, Canada

To Our Readers: We have done our best to make sure all Internet Addresses in this book were active and appropriate when we went to press. However, the author and the publisher have no control over and assume no liability for the material available on those Internet sites or on other Web sites they may link to. Any comments or suggestions can be sent by e-mail to comments@enslow.com or to the address on the back cover.

Illustration Credits: Michael W. Skrepnick

Photo Credits: American Museum of Natural History, p. 4 (top); © Corel Corporation, p. 4 (middle); Courtesy of Philip J. Currie, p. 10; Royal Tyrrell Museum, p. 4 (bottom).

Enslow Elementary
an imprint of

Enslow Publishers, Inc.
40 Industrial Road   PO Box 38
Box 398   Aldershot
Berkeley Heights, NJ 07922 Hants GU12 6BP
USA   UK
            http://www.enslow.com

CONTENTS

WORDS TO KNOW

fossils (FAH sulz)—Bones, skin, and footprints of animals that died long ago and were buried underground.

pack—A group of animals that lives and hunts together, like wolves.

museum (myoo ZEE uhm)—A building where special things are stored, studied, saved, and shown to the public.

MEET SINOSAUROPTERYX

What is that? A little dinosaur? A fuzzy little dinosaur! Meet *Sinosauropteryx* (SY noh sor AHP tur ihks).

LIVING IN A FOREST

Sinosauropteryx once lived in a forest near a lake. It hunted lizards and other small animals.

Sometimes when a *Sinosauropteryx* died, its body was buried in lake sand. After a very, very long time, the body turned into a fossil.

FINDING THE FOSSIL

In 1996, a man in China found something very important. He liked to break open rocks to look for fossils of insects and fish. One day he found something no one else had seen before.

This is where the fossil was found.

It was a fossil of a strange little dinosaur. Scientists named it *Sinosauropteryx*.

This is Mr. Li. He is pointing to the rock where he found the fossil.

IT'S A FEATHERED DINOSAUR!

feathers

Sinosauropteryx was about the size of a chicken.

The fossil had some dark marks on its back and tail. Scientists thought the marks looked a little bit like feathers.

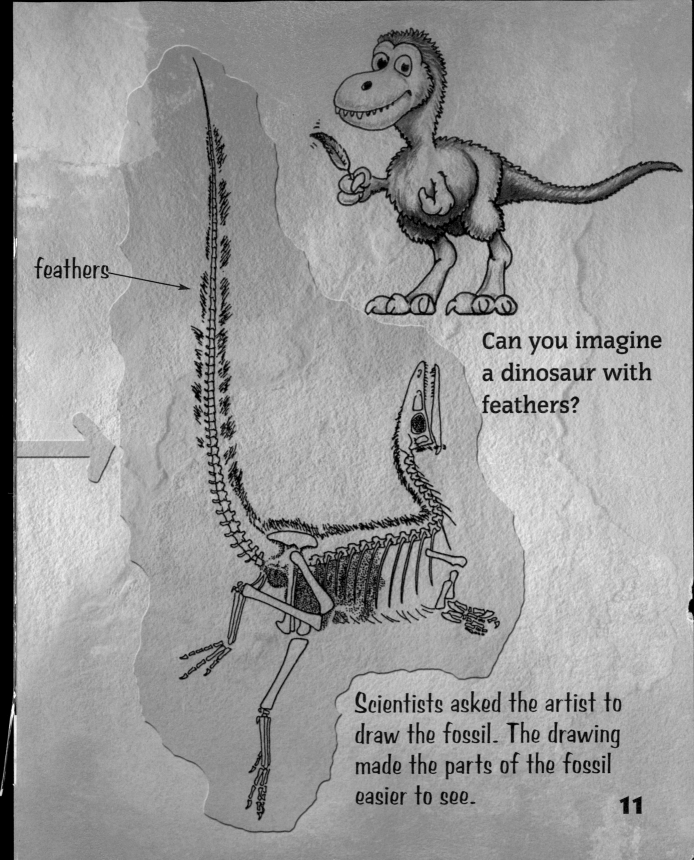

feathers

Can you imagine a dinosaur with feathers?

Scientists asked the artist to draw the fossil. The drawing made the parts of the fossil easier to see.

11

STUDYING THE FOSSIL

The *Sinosauropteryx* fossil was taken to a museum. Scientists looked at it very closely.

They could see that *Sinosauropteryx* really did have feathers all over its body. The feathers made it look like a bird.

1. Scientists asked the artist to draw pictures of the bones.

2. The artist drew muscles to cover the bones.

3. Skin and feathers were added. This shows what *Sinosauropteryx* looked like when it was alive.

S. KREPNICK

MORE FEATHERED FOSSILS

Soon, another kind of dinosaur
fossil from the forest was found.

Sinornithosaurus (SYN or nih thoh SOR us)
was also a small meat eater. It was
covered in soft, fuzzy feathers, too.
Sharp claws on its hands and feet
helped it hunt.

Sinornithosaurus moved quickly, but it could not fly.

MORE FEATHERED DINOSAURS

Scientists have now found many kinds of feathered dinosaur fossils. Packs of *Deinonychus* (dy NOH ny kuhss) hunted other larger dinosaurs.

Caudipteryx (kaw DIHP tur iks) looked like a turkey with long, skinny legs.

Bambiraptor (BAM bee rap tur) lived in North America.

17

A FLYING DINOSAUR

Guess what? Some feathered dinosaurs *could* fly. One was called *Archaeopteryx* (AHR kee AHP tur ihkz). It had teeth like a dinosaur. It had claws like a dinosaur. It looked just like other small, feathered dinosaurs.

BUT, it had long feathers on its arms. This means it could fly.

fossil of *Archaeopteryx*

So was it a dinosaur, or was it a bird? Scientists now know it was both!

DINOSAURS AND BIRDS

Over millions of years, some small dinosaurs grew longer feathers on their arms. Their arms changed into wings as they learned to fly. These feathered dinosaurs became today's birds.

Even *T. rex* babies might have had feathers to keep them warm.

SINOSAUROPTERYX FACTS

 Sinosauropteryx was the size of a chicken or small turkey.

 Sinosauropteryx feathers were for keeping warm, not for flying.

 Sinosauropteryx was found in 1996.

Sinosauropteryx lived in China.

 Sinosauropteryx had a huge thumb claw.

At least four *Sinosauropteryx* fossils have been found. They all have feathers.

LEARN MORE

BOOKS

Dodson, Peter. *An Alphabet of Dinosaurs*. New York: Scholastic Inc., 1995.

Thomson, Ruth. *Dinosaur's Day*. London: DK Publishing, Inc., 2000.

Williams, Judith. *Discovering Dinosaurs with a Fossil Hunter*. Berkeley Heights, N.J.: Enslow Publishers, Inc., 2004.

WEB SITES

The Children's Museum of Indianapolis
<http://www.childrensmuseum.org/>
Click on Dinosphere.

Discovery Kids
<http://kids.discovery.com/>
Click on Explore by Subject, then click on Dinosaur.

INDEX

About the Author

Michael W. Skrepnick is an award-winning dinosaur artist. His artwork is featured in many natural history museums and appears in scientific journals, books, and magazines. Michael lives and works in Alberta, Canada, close to some of the richest deposits of late Cretaceous dinosaur fossils in the world.

Note to Parents and Teachers: The I LIKE DINOSAURS! series supports the National Science Education Standards for K–4 science. The Words to Know section introduces subject-specific vocabulary words, including pronunciation and definitions. Early readers may need help with these new words.